P

and

Writings

of the

Báb

This book contains a selection of the prayers of the Báb and some extracts from His Writings.

More prayers and selections can be found in the following books:
Bahá'í Prayers (US edition)
Selections from the Writings of the Báb
Or online at http://www.bahai.org/library

Published by Warwick Bahá'í Bookshop 2018.
© Warwick Bahá'í Bookshop
www.warwickbahaibookshop.co.uk
Printed in UK by Clintplan.
All rights reserved.
ISBN 978-0-9957335-8-9

Cover photograph © Peter Grove.

Contents

Note to the Reader

Siyyid Alí-Muhammad was born in Iran in 1819. As a young man He realised that He was being called by God to prepare the way for the Promised One of all religions. At this point He took the title of the Báb, which means "Door" or "Gate", meaning that He was the Gateway to the Promised One. He claimed to be the "Qá'im" or "Mihdi" awaited by Muslims, the return of John the Baptist to the Christians. A similar figure is expected in many religions.

The Báb referred to the promised Messenger to come as "Him Whom God shall make manifest". He made it clear that His own message was only for a short time and that the One Who was to come was of much greater significance. Bahá'ís believe that Bahá'u'lláh ("the Glory of God") was that promised Messenger.

The Báb's mission was to prepare the way for Bahá'u'lláh and to lay the foundations for the new age and the Bahá'í Faith.

The main book of the Báb is called the Bayán, which means "Exposition". In this and other writings He praised the Messenger to come and told everyone to watch out for His coming. He instituted a new calendar, beginning in the year He declared His mission, which was 1844 in the Christian calendar (1260 in the Muslim calendar). He referred to the years 9 and 19 as being when the promised One would appear. Bahá'u'lláh received His first revelation from God in 1853 (year 9 in the Báb's calendar) but did not announce His mission publicly until 1863 (year 19).

The Báb was executed for His beliefs in 1850. Although the Báb's ministry was so short, Bahá'ís believe that His station is equal with that of Christ, Muhammad, Bahá'u'lláh, Buddha and the other Founders of great religions.

Prayers

of the Báb

Assistance

Vouchsafe unto me, O my God, the full measure of Thy love and Thy good-pleasure, and through the attractions of Thy resplendent light enrapture our hearts, O Thou Who art the Supreme Evidence and the All-Glorified. Send down upon me, as a token of Thy grace, Thy vitalising breezes, throughout the daytime and in the night season, O Lord of bounty.

No deed have I done, O my God, to merit beholding Thy face, and I know of a certainty that were I to live as long as the world lasts I would fail to accomplish any deed such as to deserve this favour, inasmuch as the station of a servant shall ever fall short of access to Thy holy precincts, unless Thy bounty should reach me and Thy tender mercy pervade me and Thy loving-kindness encompass me.

All praise be unto Thee, O Thou besides Whom there is none other God. Graciously enable me to ascend unto Thee, to be granted the honour of dwelling in Thy nearness and to have communion with Thee alone. No God is there but Thee.

Tests and Difficulties

Is there any Remover of difficulties save God? Say: Praised be God! He is God! All are His servants, and all abide by His bidding!

I adjure Thee by Thy might, O my God! Let no harm beset me in times of tests, and in moments of heedlessness guide my steps aright through Thine inspiration. Thou art God, potent art Thou to do what Thou desirest. No one can withstand Thy Will or thwart Thy Purpose.

O Lord! Thou art the Remover of every anguish and the Dispeller of every affliction. Thou art He Who banisheth every sorrow and setteth free every slave, the Redeemer of every soul. O Lord! Grant deliverance through Thy mercy, and reckon me among such servants of Thine as have gained salvation.

Thou knowest full well, O my God, that tribulations have showered upon me from all directions and that no one can dispel or transmute them except Thee. I know of a

certainty, by virtue of my love for Thee, that
Thou wilt never cause tribulations to befall any
soul unless Thou desirest to exalt his station in
Thy celestial Paradise and to buttress his heart in
this earthly life with the bulwark of Thine all-
compelling power, that it may not become
inclined toward the vanities of this world.
Indeed Thou art well aware that under all
conditions I would cherish the remembrance of
Thee far more than the ownership of all that is in
the heavens and on the earth.

Strengthen my heart, O my God, in Thine
obedience and in Thy love… Verily, I swear by
Thy glory that I yearn for naught besides
Thyself, nor do I desire anything except Thy
mercy, nor am I apprehensive of aught save Thy
justice. I beg Thee to forgive me as well as those
whom Thou lovest, howsoever Thou pleasest.
Verily, Thou art the Almighty, the Bountiful.
Immensely exalted art Thou, O Lord of the
heavens and earth, above the praise of all men,
and may peace be upon Thy faithful servants
and glory be unto God, the Lord of all the
worlds.

Detachment

Say: God sufficeth all things above all things, and nothing in the heavens or in the earth but God sufficeth. Verily, He is in Himself the Knower, the Sustainer, the Omnipotent.

O my God, my Lord and my Master! I have detached myself from my kindred and have sought through Thee to become independent of all that dwell on earth and ever ready to receive that which is praiseworthy in Thy sight. Bestow on me such good as will make me independent of aught else but Thee, and grant me an ampler share of Thy boundless favours. Verily, Thou art the Lord of grace abounding.

In the Name of Thy Lord, the Creator, the Sovereign, the All-Sufficing, the Most Exalted, He Whose help is implored by all men.
Say: O my God! O Thou Who art the Maker of the heavens and of the earth, O Lord of the Kingdom! Thou well knowest the secrets of my heart, while Thy Being is inscrutable to all save Thyself. Thou seest whatsoever is of me, while

no one else can do this save Thee. Vouchsafe unto me, through Thy grace, what will enable me to dispense with all except Thee, and destine for me that which will make me independent of everyone else besides Thee. Grant that I may reap the benefit of my life in this world and in the next. Open to my face the portals of Thy grace, and graciously confer upon me Thy tender mercy and bestowals.

O Thou Who art the Lord of grace abounding! Let Thy celestial aid surround those who love Thee, and bestow upon us the gifts and the bounties Thou dost possess. Be Thou sufficient unto us of all things, forgive our sins and have mercy upon us. Thou art Our Lord and the Lord of all created things. No one else do we invoke but Thee, and naught do we beseech but Thy favours. Thou art the Lord of bounty and grace, invincible in Thy power and the most skilful in Thy designs. No God is there but Thee, the All-Possessing, the Most Exalted.

Confer Thy blessings, O my Lord, upon the Messengers, the holy ones and the righteous. Verily, Thou art God, the Peerless, the All-Compelling.

Protection

O Lord! Unto Thee I repair for refuge, and toward all Thy signs I set my heart.
O Lord! Whether travelling or at home, and in my occupation or in my work, I place my whole trust in Thee.
Grant me then Thy sufficing help so as to make me independent of all things, O Thou Who art unsurpassed in Thy mercy!
Bestow upon me my portion, O Lord, as Thou pleasest, and cause me to be satisfied with whatsoever thou hast ordained for me.
Thine is the absolute authority to command.

Immeasurably exalted art Thou, O Lord! Protect us from what lieth in front of us and behind us, above our heads, on our right, on our left, below our feet and every other side to which we are exposed. Verily, Thy protection over all things is unfailing.

Ordain for me, O my Lord, and for those who believe in Thee that which is deemed best for us in Thine estimation, as set forth in the Mother Book, for within the grasp of Thy hand Thou holdest the determined measures of all things. Thy goodly gifts are unceasingly showered upon such as cherish Thy love, and the wondrous tokens of Thy heavenly bounties are amply bestowed on those who recognise Thy divine Unity. We commit unto Thy care whatsoever Thou hast destined for us, and implore Thee to grant us all the good that Thy knowledge embraceth.

Protect me, O my Lord, from every evil that Thine omniscience perceiveth, inasmuch as there is no power nor strength but in Thee, no triumph is forthcoming save from Thy presence, and it is Thine alone to command. Whatever God hath willed hath been, and that which He hath not willed shall not be.

There is no power nor strength except in God, the Most Exalted, the Most Mighty.

Praise

Say: God is indeed the Maker of all things. He giveth sustenance in plenty to whomsoever He willeth. He is the Creator, the Source of all beings, the Fashioner, the Almighty, the Maker, the All-Wise. He is the Bearer of the most excellent titles throughout the heavens and the earth and whatever lieth between them. All do His bidding, and all the dwellers of earth and heaven celebrate His praise, and unto Him shall all return.

All majesty and glory, O my God, and all dominion and light and grandeur and splendour be unto Thee. Thou bestowest sovereignty on whom Thou willest and dost withhold it from whom Thou desirest. No God is there but Thee, the All-Possessing, the Most Exalted. Thou art He Who createth from naught the universe and all that dwell therein. There is nothing worthy of Thee except Thyself, while all else but Thee are as outcasts in Thy holy presence and are as nothing when compared to the glory of Thine Own Being…

Glory be unto Thee, O my God, indeed no mind or vision, however keen or discriminating, can ever grasp the nature of the most insignificant of Thy signs. Verily, Thou art God, no God is there besides Thee. I bear witness that Thou Thyself alone art the sole expression of Thine attributes, that the praise of no one besides Thee can ever attain to Thy holy court nor can Thine attributes ever be fathomed by anyone other than Thyself. Glory be unto Thee, Thou art exalted above the description of anyone save Thyself, since it is beyond human conception to befittingly magnify Thy virtues or to comprehend the inmost reality of Thine Essence. Far be it from Thy glory that Thy creatures should describe Thee or that anyone besides Thyself should ever know Thee. I have known Thee, O my God, by reason of Thy making Thyself known unto me, for hadst Thou not revealed Thyself unto me, I would not have known Thee. I worship Thee by virtue of Thy summoning me unto Thee, for had it not been for Thy summons I would not have worshipped Thee…

Praised and glorified art Thou, O God! Grant that the day of attaining Thy holy presence may be fast approaching. Cheer our hearts through the potency of Thy love and good-pleasure, and bestow upon us steadfastness that we may willingly submit to Thy Will and Thy Decree. Verily, Thy knowledge embraceth all the things Thou hast created or wilt create, and Thy celestial might transcendeth whatsoever Thou hast called or wilt call into being. There is none to be worshipped but Thee, there is none to be desired except Thee, there is none to be adored besides Thee and there is naught to be loved save Thy good-pleasure.

Verily, Thou art the supreme Ruler, the Sovereign Truth, the Help in Peril, the Self-Subsisting.

Hallowed be the Lord in Whose hand is the source of dominion. He createth whatsoever He willeth by His Word of command "Be," and it is. His hath been the power of authority heretofore, and it shall remain His hereafter. He maketh victorious whomsoever He pleaseth, through the potency of His behest. He is in truth the Powerful, the Almighty. Unto Him pertaineth all glory and majesty in the kingdoms of Revelation and Creation and whatever lieth between them. Verily, He is the Potent, the All-Glorious. From everlasting He hath been the Source of indomitable strength and shall remain so unto everlasting. He is indeed the Lord of might and power. All the kingdoms of heaven and earth and whatever is between them are God's, and His power is supreme over all things. All the treasures of earth and heaven and everything between them are His, and His protection extendeth over all things. He is the Creator of the heavens and the earth and whatever lieth between them, and He truly is a witness over all things. He is the Lord of Reckoning for all that dwell in the heavens and the earth and whatever is between them. Verily, He is the Supreme Protector. He holdeth in His grasp the keys of heaven and earth and of everything between them. At His Own pleasure doth He bestow gifts, through the power of His command. Indeed His grace encompasseth all, and He is the All-Knowing.

Forgiveness

I beg Thy forgiveness, O my God, and implore pardon after the manner Thou wishest Thy servants to direct themselves to Thee. I beg of Thee to wash away our sins as befitteth Thy Lordship, and to forgive me, my parents, and those who in Thy estimation have entered the abode of Thy love in a manner which is worthy of Thy transcendent sovereignty and well beseemeth the glory of Thy celestial power. O my God! Thou hast inspired my soul to offer its supplication to Thee, and but for Thee, I would not call upon Thee. Lauded and glorified art Thou; I yield Thee praise inasmuch as Thou didst reveal Thyself unto me, and I beg Thee to forgive me, since I have fallen short in my duty to know Thee and have failed to walk in the path of Thy love.

O God our Lord! Protect us through Thy grace from whatsoever may be repugnant unto Thee, and vouchsafe unto us that which well beseemeth Thee. Give us more out of Thy bounty, and bless us. Pardon us for the things we have done, and wash away our sins, and forgive us with Thy gracious forgiveness. Verily, Thou art the Most Exalted, the Self-Subsisting.

Thy loving providence hath encompassed all created things in the heavens and on the earth, and Thy forgiveness hath surpassed the whole creation. Thine is sovereignty; in Thy hand are the Kingdoms of Creation and Revelation; in Thy right hand Thou holdest all created things, and within Thy grasp are the assigned measures of forgiveness. Thou forgivest whomsoever among Thy servants Thou pleasest. Verily, Thou art the Ever-Forgiving, the All-Loving. Nothing whatsoever escapeth Thy knowledge, and naught is there which is hidden from Thee.

O God our Lord! Protect us through the potency of Thy might, enable us to enter Thy wondrous surging ocean, and grant us that which well befitteth Thee.

Thou art the Sovereign Ruler, the Mighty Doer, the Exalted, the All-Loving.

Glory be unto Thee, O God. How can I make mention of Thee while Thou art sanctified from the praise of all mankind. Magnified be Thy Name, O God, Thou art the King, the Eternal Truth; Thou knowest what is in the heavens and on the earth, and unto Thee must all return. Thou hast sent down Thy divinely ordained Revelation according to a clear measure. Praised art Thou, O Lord! At Thy behest Thou dost render victorious whomsoever Thou willest, through the hosts of heaven and earth and whatsoever existeth between them. Thou art the Sovereign, the Eternal Truth, the Lord of invincible might.

Glorified art Thou, O Lord, Thou forgivest at all times the sins of such among Thy servants as implore Thy pardon. Wash away my sins and the sins of those who seek Thy forgiveness at dawn, who pray to Thee in the daytime and in the night season, who yearn after naught save God, who offer up whatsoever God hath graciously bestowed upon them, who celebrate Thy praise at morn and eventide, and who are not remiss in their duties.

I beg Thee to forgive me, O my Lord, for every mention but the mention of Thee, and for every praise but the praise of Thee, and for every delight but delight in Thy nearness, and for every pleasure but the pleasure of communion with Thee, and for every joy but the joy of Thy love and of Thy good-pleasure, and for all things pertaining unto me which bear no relationship unto Thee, O Thou Who art the Lord of lords, He Who provideth the means and unlocketh the doors.

Praise be unto Thee, O Lord. Forgive us our sins, have mercy upon us and enable us to return unto Thee. Suffer us not to rely on aught else besides Thee, and vouchsafe unto us, through Thy bounty, that which Thou lovest and desirest and well beseemeth Thee. Exalt the station of them that have truly believed, and forgive them with Thy gracious forgiveness. Verily, Thou art the Help in Peril, the Self-Subsisting.

The Faith of God

O Lord! Enable all the peoples of the earth to gain admittance into the Paradise of Thy Faith, so that no created being may remain beyond the bounds of Thy good-pleasure.
From time immemorial Thou hast been potent to do what pleaseth thee and transcendent above whatsoever thou desirest.

O Lord! Provide for the speedy growth of the Tree of Thy divine Unity; water it then, O Lord, with the flowing waters of Thy good-pleasure, and cause it, before the revelations of Thy divine assurance, to yield such fruits as Thou desirest for Thy glorification and exaltation, Thy praise and thanksgiving, and to magnify Thy Name, to laud the oneness of Thine Essence and to offer adoration unto Thee, inasmuch as all this lieth within Thy grasp and in that of none other. Great is the blessedness of those whose blood Thou hast chosen wherewith to water the Tree of Thine affirmation, and thus to exalt Thy holy and immutable Word.

Glory be unto Thee, O Lord, Thou Who hast brought into being all created things, through the power of Thy behest.

O Lord! Assist those who have renounced all else but Thee, and grant them a mighty victory. Send down upon them, O Lord, the concourse of the angels in the heaven and earth and all that is between, to aid Thy servants, to succour and strengthen them, to enable them to achieve success, to sustain them, to invest them with glory, to confer upon them honour and exaltation, to enrich them and to make them triumphant with a wondrous triumph.

Thou art their Lord, the Lord of the heavens and the earth, the Lord of all the worlds. Strengthen this Faith, O Lord, through the power of these servants, and cause them to prevail over all the peoples of the world; for they, of a truth, are Thy servants who have detached themselves from aught else but Thee, and Thou, verily, art the protector of true believers.

Grant Thou, O Lord, that their hearts may, through allegiance to this, thine inviolable Faith, grow stronger than anything else in the heavens and on earth and in whatsoever is between them;

and strengthen, O Lord, their hands with the tokens of Thy wondrous power that they may manifest Thy power before the gaze of all mankind.

Writings

of the Báb

The Báb's Claim

Verily I am the "Gate of God" and I give you to drink, by the leave of God, the sovereign Truth, of the crystal-pure waters of His Revelation which are gushing out from the incorruptible Fountain situate upon the Holy Mount. And those who earnestly strive after the One True God, let them then strive to attain this Gate.

Out of utter nothingness, O great and omnipotent Master, Thou hast, through the celestial potency of Thy might, brought me forth and raised me up to proclaim this Revelation. I have made none other but Thee my trust; I have clung to no will but Thy Will. Thou art, in truth, the All-Sufficing...

God beareth Me witness, I was not a man of learning, for I was trained as a merchant. In the year sixty *(1260 AH)* God graciously infused my soul with the conclusive evidences and weighty knowledge which characterise Him Who is the Testimony of God - may peace be upon Him - until finally in that year I proclaimed God's hidden Cause and unveiled its well-guarded Pillar, in such wise that no one could refute it.

Do not say, "How can He speak of God while in truth His age is no more than twenty-five?" Give ye ear unto Me. I swear by the Lord of the heavens and of the earth: I am verily a servant of God. I have been made the Bearer of irrefutable proofs from the presence of Him Who is the long-expected Remnant of God. Here is My Book before your eyes, as indeed inscribed in the presence of God in the Mother Book. God hath indeed made Me blessed, wheresoever I may be, and hath enjoined upon Me to observe prayer and fortitude so long as I shall live on earth amongst you.

God, of a truth, revealed unto Me in the sacred house of the Ka'bah, "Verily, I am God, no God is there but Me. I have singled Thee out for Myself and have chosen Thee as the Remembrance. Indeed, whosoever beareth allegiance unto Thee by walking in the way of the Báb, for him the recompense of the next world hath surely been prescribed..."

By the righteousness of God, We speak not according to selfish desire, nor hath a single letter of this Book been revealed save by the leave of God, the Sovereign Truth.

Indeed I am but a man like unto you. However, God bestoweth upon Me whatever favours He willeth as He pleaseth…

Verily I am none other but the servant of God and His Word, and none but the first one to bow down in supplication before God, the Most Exalted; and indeed God witnesseth all things.

I am, I am, I am the Promised One! I am the One Whose name you have for a thousand years invoked, at Whose mention you have risen, Whose advent you have longed to witness, and the hour of Whose Revelation you have prayed God to hasten. Verily, I say, it is incumbent upon the peoples of both the East and the West to obey My word, and to pledge allegiance to My person.

The Báb's Revelation

All praise be to God Who hath, through the power of Truth, sent down this Book unto His servant, that it may serve as a shining light for all mankind... Verily this is none other than the sovereign Truth; it is the Path which God hath laid out for all that are in heaven and on earth. Let him then who will, take for himself the right path unto his Lord. Verily this is the true Faith of God, and sufficient witness are God and such as are endowed with the knowledge of the Book.

The Bayán deriveth all its glory from Him Whom God shall make manifest.

Bear Thou witness that, through this Book, I have covenanted with all created things concerning the mission of Him Whom Thou shalt make manifest, ere the covenant concerning My own mission had been established. Sufficient witness art Thou and they that have believed in Thy signs.

The Báb's Relationship to the Promised One

Were He to appear this very moment, I would be the first to adore Him, and the first to bow down before Him.

I, Myself, am but the first servant to believe in Him and in His signs....

No allusion of Mine can allude unto Him, neither anything mentioned in the Bayán.

All that hath been exalted in the Bayán is but a ring upon My hand, and I Myself am, verily, but a ring upon the hand of Him Whom God shall make manifest - glorified be His mention! He turneth it as He pleaseth, for whatsoever He pleaseth, and through whatsoever He pleaseth. He, verily, is the Help in Peril, the Most High.

The glory of Him Whom God shall make manifest is immeasurably above every other glory, and His majesty is far above every other majesty....

The Name of the Promised One

Well is it with him who fixeth his gaze upon the Order of Bahá'u'lláh, and rendereth thanks unto his Lord. For He will assuredly be made manifest. God hath indeed irrevocably ordained it in the Bayán.

When the Daystar of Bahá will shine resplendent above the horizon of eternity it is incumbent upon you to present yourselves before His Throne. Beware lest ye be seated in His presence or ask questions without His leave. Fear ye God, O concourse of the Mirrors.

The Coming of the Promised One

In the year nine ye shall attain unto all good.

In the year nine ye will attain unto the Presence of God.

Ere nine will have elapsed from the inception of this Cause, the realities of the created things will not be made manifest.

Wait thou, until nine will have elapsed from the time of the Bayán. Then exclaim: "Blessed, therefore, be God, the most excellent of Makers!!"

After Hín *(68, i.e. 1268)* a Cause shall be given unto you which ye shall come to know.

Be attentive from the inception of the Revelation till the number of Váhíd *(19)*.

The Lord of the Day of Reckoning will be manifested at the end of Váhíd *(19)* and the beginning of eighty *(1280 A.H.)*.

The Power of the Promised One

The glory of Him Whom God shall make manifest is immeasurably above every other glory, and His majesty is far above every other majesty. His beauty excelleth every other embodiment of beauty, and His grandeur immensely exceedeth every other manifestation of grandeur. Every light paleth before the radiance of His light, and every other exponent of mercy falleth short before the tokens of His mercy. Every other perfection is as naught in face of His consummate perfection, and every other display of might is as nothing before His absolute might. His names are superior to all other names. His good-pleasure taketh precedence over any other expression of good-pleasure. His pre-eminent exaltation is far above the reach of every other symbol of exaltation. The splendour of His appearance far surpasseth that of any other appearance. His divine concealment is far more profound than any other concealment. His loftiness is immeasurably above every other loftiness. His gracious favour is unequalled by any other evidence of favour.

His power transcendeth every power. His sovereignty is invincible in the face of every other sovereignty. His celestial dominion is exalted far above every other dominion. His knowledge pervadeth all created things, and His consummate power extendeth over all beings.

Sharing the Faith of God

I, verily, have not fallen short of My duty to admonish that people. If on the day of His Revelation all that are on earth bear Him allegiance, Mine inmost being will rejoice, inasmuch as all will have attained the summit of their existence.... If not, My soul will be saddened. I truly have nurtured all things for this purpose. How, then, can anyone be veiled from Him?

It is better to guide one soul than to possess all that is on earth, for as long as that guided soul is under the shadow of the Tree of Divine Unity, he and the one who hath guided him will both be recipients of God's tender mercy, whereas possession of earthly things will cease at the time of death. The path to guidance is one of love and compassion, not of force and coercion. This hath been God's method in the past, and shall continue to be in the future!

There is no paradise more wondrous for any soul than to be exposed to God's Manifestation in His Day, to hear His verses and believe in them, to attain His presence, which is naught but the presence of God, to sail upon the sea of the heavenly kingdom of His good-pleasure, and to partake of the choice fruits of the paradise of His divine Oneness.

Wert thou to open the heart of a single soul by helping him to embrace the Cause of Him Whom God shall make manifest, thine inmost being would be filled with the inspirations of that august Name. It devolveth upon you, therefore, to perform this task in the Days of Resurrection, inasmuch as most people are helpless, and wert thou to open their hearts and dispel their doubts, they would gain admittance into the Faith of God. Therefore, manifest thou this attribute to the utmost of thine ability in the days of Him Whom God shall make manifest. For indeed if thou dost open the heart of a person for His sake, better will it be for thee than every virtuous deed; since deeds are secondary to faith in Him and certitude in His Reality.

I swear by the holy Essence of God, were all in the Bayán to unite in helping Him Whom God shall make manifest in the days of His Revelation, not a single soul, nay, not a created thing would remain on earth that would not gain admittance into Paradise. Take good heed of yourselves, for the sum total of the religion of God is but to help Him, rather than to observe, in the time of His appearance, such deeds as are prescribed in the Bayán.

Issue forth from your cities, O peoples of the West and aid God ere the Day when the Lord of mercy shall come down unto you in the shadow of the clouds with the angels circling around Him, exalting His praise and seeking forgiveness for such as have truly believed in Our signs. Verily His decree hath been issued, and the command of God, as given in the Mother Book, hath indeed been revealed...

Recognition of the Promised One

O servants of God! Be ye patient, for, God grant, He Who is the sovereign Truth will suddenly appear amongst you, invested with the power of the mighty Word…

At the time of the manifestation of Him Whom God shall make manifest everyone should be well trained in the teachings of the Bayán, so that none of the followers may outwardly cling to the Bayán and thus forfeit their allegiance unto Him. If anyone does so, the verdict of "disbeliever in God" shall be passed upon him.

…on the Day of Resurrection God will ask every one of his understanding and not of his following in the footsteps of others. How often a person, having inclined his ears to the holy verses, would bow down in humility and would embrace the Truth, while his leader would not do so. Thus every individual must bear his own responsibility, rather than someone else bearing it for him. At the time of the appearance of Him Whom God will make manifest the most distinguished among the learned and the lowliest of men shall both be judged alike. How often the most insignificant of men have acknowledged the truth, while the most learned have remained wrapt in veils.

How vast the number of people who are well versed in every science, yet it is their adherence to the holy Word of God which will determine their faith, inasmuch as the fruit of every science is none other than the knowledge of divine precepts and submission unto His good-pleasure.

Better is it for a person to write down but one of His verses than to transcribe the whole of the Bayán and all the books which have been written in the Dispensation of the Bayán. For everything shall be set aside except His Writings, which will endure until the following Revelation. And should anyone inscribe with true faith but one letter of that Revelation, his recompense would be greater than for inscribing all the heavenly Writings of the past and all that has been written during previous Dispensations. Likewise continue thou to ascend through one Revelation after another, knowing that thy progress in the Knowledge of God shall never come to an end, even as it can have no beginning.

Say, by reason of your remembering Him Whom God shall make manifest and by extolling His name, God will cause your hearts to be dilated with joy, and do ye not wish your hearts to be in such a blissful state? Indeed the hearts of them that truly believe in Him Whom God shall make manifest are vaster than the expanse of heaven and earth and whatever is between them. God hath left no hindrance in their hearts, were it but the size of a mustard seed. He will cheer their hearts, their spirits, their souls and their bodies and their days of prosperity or adversity, through the exaltation of the name of Him Who is the supreme Testimony of God and the promotion of the Word of Him Who is the Dayspring of the glory of their Creator.

The Eternal Cycle of Messengers

The Lord of the universe hath never raised up a prophet nor hath He sent down a Book unless He hath established His covenant with all men, calling for their acceptance of the next Revelation and of the next Book; inasmuch as the outpourings of His bounty are ceaseless and without limit.

True knowledge, therefore, is the knowledge of God, and this is none other than the recognition of His Manifestation in each Dispensation. … This doth not mean, however, that one ought not to yield praise unto former Revelations. … had the religion taught by Adam not existed, this Faith would not have attained its present stage. Thus consider thou the development of God's Faith until the end that hath no end.

With each and every Prophet Whom We have sent down in the past, We have established a separate Covenant concerning the Remembrance of God and His Day.

Thy Lord hath never raised up a prophet in the past who failed to summon the people to His Lord, and today is truly similar to the times of old, were ye to ponder over the verses revealed by God.

Verily God will raise up Him Whom God shall make manifest, and after Him Whomsoever He willeth, even as He hath raised up prophets before the Point of the Bayán. He in truth hath power over all things.

Unto every people We have sent down the Book in their own language. This Book We have, verily, revealed in the language of Our Remembrance and it is in truth a wondrous language.

The Day of God

O my servants! This is God's appointed Day which the merciful Lord hath promised you in His Book...

Assuredly we are today living in the Days of God. These are the glorious days on the like of which the sun hath never risen in the past. These are the days which the people in bygone times eagerly expected. What hath then befallen you that ye are fast asleep? These are the days wherein God hath caused the Daystar of Truth to shine resplendent. What hath then caused you to keep your silence? These are the appointed days which ye have been yearningly awaiting in the past -- the days of the advent of divine justice. Render ye thanks unto God, O ye concourse of believers.

O peoples of the earth! Verily the resplendent Light of God hath appeared in your midst, invested with this unerring Book, that ye may be guided aright to the ways of peace and, by the leave of God, step out of the darkness into the light and onto this far-extended Path of Truth...

Spiritual Guidance

<u>Worship</u>

The most acceptable prayer is the one offered with the utmost spirituality and radiance; its prolongation hath not been and is not beloved by God. The more detached and the purer the prayer, the more acceptable is it in the presence of God.

Worship thou God in such wise that if thy worship lead thee to the fire, no alteration in thine adoration would be produced, and so likewise if thy recompense should be paradise. Thus and thus alone should be the worship which befitteth the one True God. Shouldst thou worship Him because of fear, this would be unseemly in the sanctified Court of His presence, and could not be regarded as an act by thee dedicated to the Oneness of His Being. Or if thy gaze should be on paradise, and thou shouldst worship Him while cherishing such a hope, thou wouldst make God's creation a partner with Him, notwithstanding the fact that paradise is desired by men.

Fire and paradise both bow down and prostrate themselves before God. That which is worthy of His Essence is to worship Him for His sake, without fear of fire, or hope of paradise.

<u>Purity</u>

God loveth those who are pure. Naught in the Bayán and in the sight of God is more loved than purity and immaculate cleanliness....

This World and the Next

Say, this earthly life shall come to an end, and everyone shall expire and return unto my Lord God Who will reward with the choicest gifts the deeds of those who endure with patience. Verily thy God assigneth the measure of all created things as He willeth, by virtue of His behest; and those who conform to the good-pleasure of your Lord, they are indeed among the blissful.

All men have proceeded from God and unto Him shall all return. All shall appear before Him for judgement. He is the Lord of the Day of Resurrection, of Regeneration and of Reckoning, and His revealed Word is the Balance.

True death is realised when a person dieth to himself at the time of His Revelation in such wise that he seeketh naught except Him. True resurrection from the sepulchres means to be quickened in conformity with His Will, through the power of His utterance.

Paradise is attainment of His good-pleasure and everlasting hell-fire His judgement through justice.

The Day He revealeth Himself is Resurrection Day which shall last as long as He ordaineth. Everything belongeth unto Him and is fashioned by Him. All besides Him are His creatures.

Obedience to the Laws of God

There is no paradise, in the estimation of the believers in the Divine Unity, more exalted than to obey God's commandments, and there is no fire in the eyes of those who have known God and His signs, fiercer than to transgress His laws and to oppress another soul, even to the extent of a mustard seed.

Fix your gaze upon Him Whom God shall make manifest in the Day of Resurrection, then firmly believe in that which is sent down by Him.

<u>Unity</u>

Become as true brethren in the one and indivisible religion of God, free from distinction, for verily God desireth that your hearts should become mirrors unto your brethren in the Faith, so that ye find yourselves reflected in them, and they in you.

God hath, at all times and under all conditions, been wholly independent of His creatures. He hath cherished and will ever cherish the desire that all men may attain His gardens of Paradise with utmost love, that no one should sadden another, not even for a moment, and that all should dwell within His cradle of protection and security ….